# Contents:

CW01426265

# Introduction

One of the most popular chapters in the book "Bad Dog to Best Friend", this is a step-by-step guide to weaning your dog from a crate and teaching him to stay home alone with full run of the house. It was inspired by the true story of a semi-adult shelter dog who used the house as her own personal potty and chew toy. If she can be taught to stay home alone without chewing or potty in the house, there's hope for your dog, too.

We've included the chapters on potty training and dog chewing as you can't deal with one without tackling all three. The full version of the book has 26 chapters. This guide is a 3-chapter excerpt from the full version, which is available in both paperback and Kindle on Amazon.

# Potty Training a Problem Dog

*One problem solved, many more to go*
*(Adrift in a sea of dog pee, I saw a glimmer of hope)*

Now that we'd solved the workday problem we were back to Dakota's bad habit of peeing in the house when she wasn't in the crate - which was anytime we were home with her. Dakota didn't give a lot of warning before she peed. She didn't sniff or circle looking for the perfect place. She simply stopped in mid-stride without warning, squatted and peed all in about one second. Dakota was that quick.

We trained her to pee outdoors by using food as a bribe. Dakota had an insatiable craving for food and we used this in her training. We bought a bag of large kibble dog food different from her normal food. Every time she peed outdoors we gave her a piece of food as a reward. You'd think it was a hunk of steak the way she coveted that potty treat and she quickly learned to pee outdoors. The trouble was - she still peed indoors. No matter how often we took her out we couldn't seem to stop her from peeing indoors. It seemed hopeless.

**I'LL TRY TO BE A GOOD DOG, I PROMISE!**

The dog experts pretty much all agree that it's better to train your dog with a reward system than a fear system so we tried to focus on the potty treats. We made it clear to her that we were not pleased when she peed indoors but we had to be very careful not to yell because if we raised our voice even one iota, it stressed her out and made her pee again.

Those days were difficult. Even when she knew we were taking her out for potty she'd get excited and it just came out before we could actually get her through the door. We gave a stern *no* when she slipped up, immediately took her out and if she peed again outdoors, she got a reward. I hated giving her that potty treat if she'd peed in the house first. It felt like I was rewarding her for bad behavior but I was following the advice from the dog experts.

The hardest times were in the evenings when we came home from work. Dakota had held it all day and she was fully loaded. We kept the dog crate next to the door in the hopes of getting her out of the house before she let loose. In the beginning it didn't work. The minute her feet cleared the door to the crate the pee was coming out. We continued as fast as we could out to the backyard with Dakota peeing all the way down the stairs. We took her directly to the pee pee spot where she peed even more. Dakota's bladder seemed to be an eternal spring which never stopped flowing.

Mornings were dicey as well. She'd held it all night long and woke up fully loaded. I never delayed in taking her out in the morning. I'd throw on a bathrobe and get her out the door as quickly as possible, not even taking time for my own morning potty.

There were times when it felt hopeless. We thought we'd never get her to stop peeing indoors. Ten weeks after adopting Dakota - putting her at almost ten months old - we finally had a breakthrough. For the first time ever I did not take Dakota out immediately after getting up in the morning. I took a few minutes for my own potty and to get fully dressed before taking her out and still she held it. That showed incredible progress for her.

After ten weeks of diligent potty training she was not only holding it all night, Dakota had progressed from peeing many times a day in the house to only once or twice a month. We no longer had to keep the carpet shampooer out in the middle of the room ready to fire up. We were able to stash it back in the closet where it belonged - hidden and out of our way. Dakota had truly made incredible progress and we were hopeful that she'd eventually be accident-free.

We'd learned several tricks of the trade in dealing with Dakota's potty problem. It wasn't enough to simply reward her for pottying outdoors. We needed to anticipate what caused her to pee in the house and nip it in the bud - staying one step ahead of her at all times. We needed to teach her new habits to replace the old, bad habits. Most of all we had to have patience. That was the hardest part.

### Tricks of the trade
### (Techniques for potty training)
#### During the night

It's normal for me to get up several times during the night so when I got up for my own needs, I'd throw on a bathrobe and take Dakota out. Even during those horrible first weeks Dakota never once peed in the bedroom at night. That in itself was amazing. Still, I took her out not wanting to push my luck. Hauling out the carpet shampooer in the dead of night did not appeal to me.

Once I saw that she seemed willing to hold it at night, I cut back from three times a night to two times, then down to one time, then finally not at all. However, the moment I'd wake up in the morning I'd rush her down the stairs and out the door. I didn't dare make her wait, even for me to go pee. I figured if she'd been good enough to hold it all night I wasn't about to tempt the fates.

### You're with me

In the early days I kept Dakota with me at all times in the house. I literally made her follow me around the house as I went about my day. If I was going upstairs I'd hook my finger under her collar and guide her up the stairs with me saying *you're with me*. This became our daily routine. The goal was to keep her under my supervision at all times so that if she showed any signs of potty in the house (or any other bad behavior) I could immediately nip it in the bud.

This was pretty effective overall in her training. It also produced an unexpected result. She learned the command *you're with me* simply by repetition. I wasn't trying to teach her the words. I just simply said them anytime I made her stay with me and eventually, anytime I left the room or said those words she would immediately follow. It became her habit to follow me around the house. She also learned my very predictable routine and knew that on certain days she was going to spend the day upstairs with me as I worked at the computer. She eventually graduated to having freedom of whatever floor I was on without needing constant supervision. On those days she would snooze in the bedroom.

### Location, location

We kept the dog crate next to the door to minimize the time it took to get her out the door on our workdays after she'd held it all day. This was an important step. Once she was able to hold it until she got all the way out to the potty spot, we moved the crate farther from the door. If she slipped up, the crate went back to the original location for a week or so. Forwards and backwards, that's how we progressed.

### Potty treats

We rewarded Dakota with potty treats when she peed outdoors. We went through so many potty treats that we didn't use fancy schmancy expensive treats - we used one single piece of dog food. Her normal food came in small pieces and the potty treats were much bigger and a different flavor. For Dakota, that one nugget was enough to excite her and we kept a bowl of potty treats near the back door.

It didn't take long for Dakota to expect a potty treat for peeing outdoors. Once she got the hang of it and peed outdoors on command, I started delaying the treat until she was back in the house. This paved the way for other types of training later on.

After we fenced in the backyard I was able to let her out unsupervised and reward her for coming back after pottying. In other words, the potty treat eventually became a reward for coming back rather than a reward for pottying outdoors. Once indoors she'd sit next to the door and wait for the treat. I'd say *catch* and toss it to her. She learned to catch the potty treat in midair and she learned a new word.

Several weeks later when Dakota started losing interest in the nuggets of dog food we switched to raw, peeled baby carrots. Initially she was hesitant over this new edible but once she'd eaten a couple, she fully embraced the carrots and they became a desirable treat for her.

Dog owners often overlook potential treats that don't fit the standard concept of a hunk of meat or a piece of cheese. There are a number of raw vegetables that your dog might embrace if you give it half a chance. Raw carrots, cabbage hearts and broccoli stems are some of the treats we give our dogs.

Be aware that there are foods you should never give your dog: garlic, onions, chocolate, macadamia nuts, avocados, grapes and raisins. They can make your dog very sick or potentially kill your dog. Contrary to popular belief, raw meat and eggs can harm your dog as well. Dogs are just as susceptible to salmonella and e-coli as we are. Moldy foods should also be avoided. If it isn't fresh enough for you to eat, you shouldn't give it to your dog.

### Water restrictions

In the beginning we restricted Dakota's water intake. I searched the internet high and low for specific recommendations on how much water we should be giving her. While it was easy to find information on how much food she should get, I couldn't find a single reference as to how much water she should drink in a day.

One of the dog training shows on television had an episode about dogs peeing in the house and the dog in question was a tiny little dog. The owners made sure that the dog had a full bowl of water at all times. The dog expert demonstrated why this was causing their dog to pee in the house.

The dog expert held up a small glass and said, "This is the size of your dog's bladder..." Then she lined up how many glasses of water the dog actually drank in a day. "...and this is how much water you are giving your dog every day. How can you expect him to hold all these glasses of water with his tiny little bladder?"

Dakota's water bowl held two 8-ounce glasses of water. I had no idea how big her bladder was but I knew that she weighed about 60 pounds. I weigh more than twice that and I should consume 6-8 glasses of water in a day so by those calculations the most Dakota should have been getting was 3-4 glasses full per day.

Attempting to compare her needs to my own was prone to error as I was using the 6-8 glasses for humans calculation based on what I'd always been told. This offered no differentiation between a human who weighed 100 pounds versus a human who weighed 250 pounds but it was the best I had to work with.

I started out giving her 8 ounces in the morning and 8 ounces in the evening on our workdays when nobody would be here to take her out during the day. On days we'd be home I'd give her an additional 4 ounces or so about midday. I didn't give her any after dinner because I wanted to make sure she was empty before bedtime. Planning for long stretches of hours when you won't be taking them outside for potty is important. You can compensate by giving more water when you are able to take them out more frequently.

As Dakota learned to hold her pee I increased the quantity of water. If I increased it too much and she peed on the carpet then the next day I'd go to a smaller quantity again. This was trial and error. If I gave her *this much* she would pee - if I gave her *that much* she wouldn't pee.

After 10 months of potty training I was giving her three to four 8-ounce glasses full on days when I was home, and up to 2.5 glasses full on our workdays. To put this in perspective I worked out of the house 2 days a week and at home 3 days a week, so five days a week I was able to take her out more often which allowed me to give her a lot more water on those five days. Eventually I was able to stop measuring and just fill her water bowl when it was empty - even before leaving her for nine hours on a workday.

### Go directly to jail - do not pass go

If Dakota peed out of excitement or stress we did not punish her. We made it very clear that we were displeased but we did not put any consequences onto it. However, if she peed out of spite, we did punish her. We took her outside to let her finish the job and then we put her in the dog crate for an hour or so. We thought of it as jail time for bad behavior.

The dog experts tell you not to ever use the dog crate as a punishment so we went against their advice. Those first months were so bad and her pee problem was so severe that we simply tried every method we could think of to break that horrible habit of hers - and that's exactly what it is, a very bad habit.

How can you tell what kind of pee it is? How can you tell the difference between a stress pee, an excited pee, and a spiteful pee? Consider the circumstances that led up to it. If you're playing ball with your dog in the house and he squats and pees then this is an excited pee. If you walk in the door after being gone for many hours and he pees then this, too, is an excited pee. If he did something wrong and you've just chastised him it might be a stress pee or it might be a spiteful pee.

**DAKOTA WITH A COCKY ATTITUDE**

We learned to read Dakota's body language to determine whether she was stressed, happy, or mad at us. This is important if you'll be using different strategies depending on your dog's reason for the wrongdoing.

If Dakota was stressed, her eyes looked worried and she was breathing hard. If she was cocky or mad her demeanor was full of attitude, bad attitude, and it showed. The spiteful pees almost always occurred if she'd been bullying Gypsy Rose and got in trouble for it.

### Rubbing her nose in it

Yes, on a few occasions we attempted to rub her nose in the pee even though the dog experts tell you not to. If we knew she was doing it out of spite we did try to rub her nose in it, but you just try to take a 60 pound dog and force their nose to the floor when they stiffen their legs and use every muscle against you. Good luck with that.

### Paper training and pee pads

We did not attempt to paper train Dakota or teach her to potty on pee pads. This would have been counter-productive. The objective was to teach her to pee outside - not train her to pee inside. Paper training and pee pad training teach your dog to pee indoors. While this might be okay for a small dog who pees in tiny puddles it would have been disastrous for a dog like Dakota who put out large quantities of urine, especially when we were trying to break her of the habit of peeing indoors.

### Go pee pee

I used the phrase *go pee pee* every time she peed outdoors and the phrase *go poopie* every time she pooped. She quickly learned the meaning of both phrases. I also taught her the word *no* as an overall word of disapproval for whatever she was doing. The more words your dog knows the better your relationship will be. Not only was I able to tell Dakota when I wanted her to go pee, I was able to communicate to her that potty in the house was bad.

You need to be able to communicate with your dog to tell them what you want, otherwise they won't know. Dogs aren't mind readers. The added benefit of knowing the difference between the two types of potty allowed us greater control of our dogs' potty habits when we took them on road trips.

### Don't get her over-excited in the house

To cut down on the excited potty accidents we did not play with Dakota in the house. We did not throw the ball, wrestle with her or play tug of war. We did not do anything in the house to get her all revved up and excited. The goal was to remove the reasons she did it in the house in order to give us time to create better potty habits in her. This was one of the most difficult rules we had to follow. Dakota was young and full of energy and she needed to play. It was hard not to play with her indoors but there was just no way around it - at least not in the beginning.

All we could do for Dakota in the house was to calmly pet her or give her chew toys to keep her busy, much like giving a baby a pacifier. Dakota went through a lot of chewies in those first months with us. We gave her hard bones, rawhide bones and cow hooves to chew on. The dog experts are against all of these chewies with good reason, but for Dakota's early days with us it was a risk that we needed to take. The dangers of giving your dog chewies is a subject for a later chapter.

### Empty the dog

As Dakota's potty accidents became less and less frequent we gradually began playing with her briefly indoors. It was critical to take her out for potty before attempting to play with her in the house. We called this *Emptying the Dog*. If we forgot it was almost a guarantee that she'd let loose on the carpeting during play. Dakota was never truly empty but it helped. I'd never seen a dog that could pee as much as Dakota could - she stayed fully loaded. She peed so much that we had the vet test her for kidney and bladder problems but they found no medical problems and declared her to be in perfect health.

The concept was simple: We'd empty the dog, play with her in the house for a few brief moments and then take her outside for potty before she got to the pee point. There was a lot of guesswork involved as to when that point would come and we often relied on her body language.

Sometimes Dakota would stop in mid-play to sniff the floor as if she thought she'd had an accident and was checking. Sometimes it was in the way she held her back-end as if she were clenching. The signs were often subtle and we could never be certain but if we were in the least bit concerned, out she'd go for a potty break.

The back door became a revolving door - in and out and in and out as we tried to keep her as empty as possible. I worried that we were taking her out too often and that she was playing us to get a potty treat.

By the time she was two years old she did achieve the golden goal of being able to play rambunctiously in the house without letting loose. This was a long time coming but she did finally get there and today, we don't need to restrict her indoor play. We do, however, still empty the dog when we're getting ready for high excitement play.

### Who dictates potty time?

Dakota adopted the habit of sitting or laying by the back door when she wanted to go out. Initially we honored such requests but this was a sticky point. On the one hand we wanted her to learn that potty outdoors was the only good potty; on the other hand I did not want to teach Dakota to be a bothersome Boss Dog who dictated her potty times to me. I wanted Dakota to learn that if she is indoors, she does not potty *ever*, and to hold it until we take her outdoors. I wanted her to learn that outdoors was on my timetable, not hers. Allowing your dog to dictate potty time is the same as allowing your dog to be Boss Dog. This is a dog who is allowed to rule the roost which opens up a whole slew of problems in itself.

Because of Dakota's severe potty issues we ended up compromising. In the evenings when we were watching television we did honor her requests to go out but under no circumstances did I allow her to wake me up from sleeping or disturb me during work at home hours. Oddly enough she never pestered me to go out when I was working from home. She seemed perfectly willing to hold it.

She held it all night during sleep hours, she held it all day if she was in the dog crate, and she held it when I was working at home - so why was she so all-fired willing to let loose during the evening hours?

There wasn't a single square inch of carpeting that hadn't been peed on. The main difference in the evening hours was that Dakota went into excited play mode and she had access to our other dog Gypsy Rose. These two activities put her into high gear. She was also more likely to get into trouble and be chastised for doing something wrong in the evening. Learning your dog's triggers can help you to figure out how not to trip the trigger and eventually work toward teaching your dog not to react to the trigger at all.

Once we knew she could hold it we stopped taking her out every time she asked which was several times in the course of a normal evening. I started telling her *we did that already* as a way of saying no, I'm not taking you out again, and she'd give up the vigil at the door.

### How long does it take to potty train an adult dog?
### (Or... when can I put the mop away?)

The dog experts tell you that potty training a puppy takes two weeks and that it can take up to six weeks to potty train an adult dog. We did not find this true for Dakota. Even with her level of intelligence it took many months to retrain her not to pee in the house. While she quickly learned to pee outdoors, and to pee on command outdoors, she still slipped up every time she was excited or stressed which was often during those first few months.

Dakota had to learn to trust us, to trust that this home wouldn't be yanked out from under her and to trust that even if we were displeased with her it did not mean she'd be dragged off to the dog pound. Yo-yo dogs come with a lot of mental baggage and this affects their training curve. With every week that passed her slip ups were less and less frequent. Dakota was improving.

Eight months after adopting her she was finally holding her pee even when highly excited but on occasion, if she was stressed, she'd still have an accident.

After ten months of potty training and diligently working with her to break the bad habits and establish new, good habits, Dakota had transformed from a dog who peed on the carpet several times a day to only once or twice a month. She had progressed. She no longer peed in the house from excitement. The rare occasion when she did slip up was almost always because she was mad at us.

Still we made sure to empty the dog before we played with her in the house. This was one of our golden rules and it held us in good stead with her. Dakota was an incredibly happy dog and as time passed and she learned more good habits, our moments with her started to bring us pleasure instead of constant work and frustration.

Our time with Dakota became a source of great happiness and joy and we were finally reaping the rewards of our hard work. Life was good.

# Dealing With Dog Chewing Problems

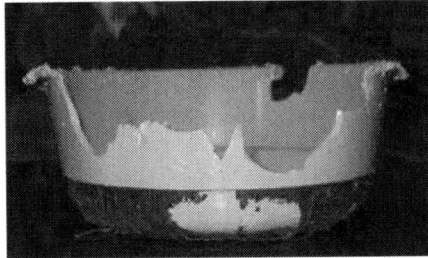

DAKOTA'S CHEWED UP FOOD BOWL
*What had we gotten ourselves into?*
*(And how do we get out of it?)*

How do you transform a dog who chews your world to pieces? Along with the many other problems we'd inherited with Dakota, she chewed things.

Three days after adopting her we had to go to work which meant leaving her home alone for the day. We confined her to a portion of the garage with food, water and dog toys. My husband got home first and nothing could have prepared him for what he walked into. Dakota had pooped everywhere. Not only had she pooped, she had managed to smear it all over herself, the floor, dog food bowl, water dispenser, and the dog toys we'd left for her.

Subsequent days we came home to find that she'd chewed her dog bowls into teeny little pieces and had ripped open a bag of cement, scattering its contents hither and yon.

About a month after adopting Dakota we got her a dog crate and moved her into the house on our workdays. This solved some of her problems such as the barking all day but she still chewed. We attempted to put a blanket in the crate but the very first day she chewed a two foot hole in it so we took it out and she didn't get another one. We did not attempt to put dog food or water bowls in the crate. We already knew how they would fare. We fed and watered her before we left and again when we got home. That was just going to have to be good enough.

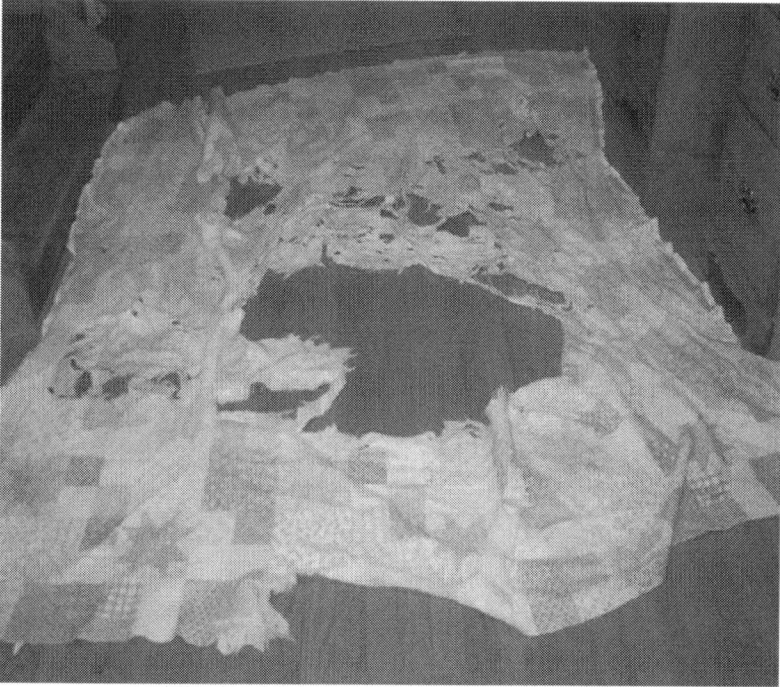

DAKOTA'S BLANKET WITH HOLES CHEWED IN IT

Several months later we went off on another vacation. It wasn't a dog vacation so both dogs stayed home in the garage with a neighbor to look after them. We bought a 6x10 chain link dog kennel and put it in the garage for Dakota. With her habit of bullying Gypsy Rose we wanted to keep them separate. We left Dakota with an automatic water dispenser, a heavy plastic dog food bowl, and we laid a thick carpet of hay down for her. We arranged for the girl next door to feed her twice a day.

## Why do dogs chew?
### (Figure out the why and you're halfway to the solution)

Within 24 hours Dakota had destroyed the water dispenser. In spite of our efforts to make her comfortable, being in the garage stressed her and she dealt with stress by chewing.

**CHEWED UP BASE OF WATER DISPENSER**

Dogs chew for a variety of reasons. A dog who is bored might be looking for a way to entertain themselves. Sometimes dog play gets a little rambunctious and objects get destroyed. Some dogs don't do well when left alone for too many hours. Some dogs even have issues if you ignore them a lot when you're at home.

Active breeds like herding dogs and sporting dogs need to be kept busy. If you don't provide them with outlets for their energy they will make their own outlets. Young dogs of any breed are full of energy and if you don't exercise them, all of that pent up energy will find a way out - usually in a bad way. Dogs don't even start to calm down until they're about three.

Dakota was all of the above. She had abandonment fears so whenever we left her she became distressed. Being an Australian Cattle Dog/Siberian Husky mix put her in the high energy working dog category. In addition, Dakota was young and full of energy.

*Would you trust a toddler to his own devices?*
*(Then why do you trust your dog?)*

Dakota was a chewer. She reminded us of a baby bird. Her mouth was always open with the expectation of latching onto something and if it sensed an object nearby, it attempted to grab onto the object. I don't think she consciously thought about it. Her mouth seemed to be a live thing unto itself. If something came into the range of her mouth, she latched onto it and started to chew. It wasn't malicious - it just was.

In the early days we learned not to leave Dakota alone in the house out of sight. If she disappeared around a corner I was hot on her tail. Not only did she chew but Dakota was in her curious stage, exploring the world around her like a young child discovering the wonders of the world for the first time.

Parents with young toddlers often child-proof their homes making sure to cover electrical outlets, move glass objects off of low tables, install child-proof locks on low cupboards, use baby gates, put hook locks high up on screen doors, and so forth. The goal is to protect the child from injury and to prevent your home from being destroyed by an innocent child who simply doesn't understand that knocking a glass vase off the table and breaking it is bad. It takes years to teach a child the many rules of life and in the meantime you must watch over him.

Your dog is no different. Dogs don't know that chewing on electrical cords can kill them any more than toddlers do. Dogs aren't born into the world knowing that a table leg isn't something for them to chew on. Consider this: A dog in nature will chew on tree branches and to your dog, the table leg is just another piece of wood. You must teach your dog just as you would a child: object by object. Don't leave your dog alone unsupervised with run of the house until you are confident that they can be trusted not to injure themselves or damage your home.

As Dakota explored this new world which was our home we had to teach her, object by object, which items were taboo for her. At various times she grabbed an empty plastic milk jug, shoes, a wooden billy club, tin foil with meat drippings from the garbage can, berries off of potted plants (which is a dangerous habit if the berries happen to be poisonous), and a roll of toilet tissue sitting on the floor. We didn't catch her in time with the toilet tissue and she shredded it.

During those first months we kept her in our sight at all times. We never left her unsupervised in the house - ever. I made her follow me everywhere, hooking my finger under her collar and guiding her around the house with me as I moved from room to room.

If I was doing dishes, I made her stay in the kitchen with me. If we were in the living room watching television, she was expected to stay in the living room with us. When taking a shower, I took her into the bathroom with me and closed the door so that she couldn't leave. I blocked the stairway so that she had to stay on whatever floor I was on.

Wherever I went, I took Dakota with me and if she attempted to leave the room, I immediately went after her and brought her back in. We didn't ever yell at her for leaving the room - we simply prevented it. With the constant repetition of bringing her back in she got the message to stay close to us. She got the message not to leave the room. Dogs learn by repetition and if you are consistent, they will get the message.

## *Bait and Switch*
### *(I'll trade you this dog bone for that smelly old shoe)*

I wanted to catch Dakota the minute she grabbed something in her mouth so that I could tell her if it was legal or not. The goal was to teach her that unless it was something that we gave to her, she shouldn't touch it, and we were very careful in what we did give her.

This is where many people fail. If you play tug-of-war with an old sock you are teaching your dog that socks are legal toys. If your dog has his own teddy bear he may not realize that other teddy bears belonging to your children are taboo. If you tease him with a broom when you are sweeping, don't be surprised if your broom becomes his next chew toy. Your choices will impact your dog's behavior so give thought to the items you allow your dog to have.

**DAKOTA CHEWING A GIGANTIC RAWHIDE BONE**

If Dakota grabbed something illegal, I immediate took it away and made it clear that this object was forbidden and replaced it with something that she was allowed to have. If I took something away, I gave her something else to replace it. In other words, you don't just take away the bad thing - this can cause a tantrum just as with a child. Instead, you trade it for something else. Dakota learned which items belonged to her. We went through a lot of dog chewies during that first year.

We gave her hard bones, rawhide bones and hooves to chew on. The dog experts are against all of these chewies but we had to divert her from chewing our house to pieces.

### Dog treats can kill a dog
### (Even the ones you buy at the pet store)

Why are the dog experts against these types of chewies? They can actually harm your dog. Small shards can break off of a hoof or bone and if your dog swallows a piece with sharp points, it can pierce your dog's stomach or intestinal lining and kill him. If your dog swallows a piece of rawhide or hoof that's too big it can block the intestines and require surgery to remove, if it doesn't kill your dog first.

Even small pieces of rawhide can be dangerous. Rawhide swells up when wet so what was a small piece going down becomes a much bigger piece once inside. Neither rawhide nor cow hooves break down quickly once ingested so they can linger and build up with subsequent swallowings.

A solid mass of any substance can cause an internal blockage that is fatal to your dog. If you don't believe me do a Google search. Type in "dangerous dog treats" or "dog treats kill" and you'll find page after page of scary stuff - some of it from trustworthy sources such as news networks CNN, NBC and ABC.

If Dakota hadn't been so difficult, if she'd not had so many needs and problems to solve, we probably wouldn't have given her such treats once we knew the dangers. Like most dog owners, however, we didn't know any of this when we adopted her and I'm not sure what we could have done differently. Safe treats don't offer much to a dog who needs to chew. We learned about the dangers the hard way and thankfully she survived her first brush with death.

One night she gave us quite a scare. It was related to swallowing the remnants of a hoof. Dakota didn't usually stop eating her chewies until she'd ingested too much so we had to watch to see how much she was actually swallowing. If we thought she was swallowing too much we took the chewy away.

Because of this Dakota became paranoid. She knew that sooner or later we'd take away her chewy so any movement on our part, such as getting up to go to the kitchen for a drink of water, was suspect to her. She'd hurry up and try to eat as quickly as she could, often swallowing big chunks in the process.

One night she'd gotten down to the last remnants of a cow hoof - a piece that was about two inches around. She saw me coming towards her and before I could snag the hoof she swallowed it whole. I didn't know at the time how big a piece she had swallowed. It wasn't until it came out the other end that I had an inkling of the size. All I knew was that she'd swallowed a piece when she saw me coming and I was pretty sure it was a big piece.

Not long after, Dakota became ill. She tried to drink water but it immediately came back out as a projectile - Dakota was vomiting like a scene from *The Exorcist* movie. It was as if the water never got fully down into her innards before it came up again and I suspected that the chewy had created a blockage. She seemed to be breathing okay and her main distress appeared to be the inability to hold down water so I did not take her to the vet, hoping that it would work its way through her. You just never know when something is serious and you simply have to make a judgement call - hopefully the right one.

I stayed up with her all night, taking her out to the bathroom several times in the hopes that it would move through her system. She was agitated and pacing most of the night, wanting water and wanting to go out to the bathroom.

After an exhausting night she finally passed the chunk of hoof. I poked sticks in her poop searching for the evidence. I found a two inch round hard object which I assumed to be the remnants of the hoof she had swallowed the night before. Once she passed it, she was fine. Her distress was gone and the incident did not appear to have left permanent damage. Finally able to rest, we both slept most of that day.

Dogs die from swallowing objects that block their intestines. If the object had gotten stuck inside of her, only surgery would have saved her. We took a big risk by not taking Dakota to the vet. I did stay up with her that night, giving her whatever she asked for such as going out for potty every hour or so. I prayed that her efforts to move it would be successful and fortunately, they were.

After the big scare we watched Dakota like a hawk. If small pieces broke off her bones or hooves we immediately took the pieces away and disposed of them. If her chewy got down to that dangerous size where swallowing it whole might cause a blockage, we tossed the chewy and gave her a new one. No matter what else we were doing we kept one eye on Dakota with her chewy, monitoring for both how much she ingested and for big pieces. Losing Dakota just wasn't an option. In spite of all her problems we'd grown to love her dearly.

Rawhides weren't quite as bad but they didn't last long. Dakota could devour an average size rawhide bone in an hour. This was bad not only for her innards but it didn't keep her teeth busy long enough. We needed to keep her in chewy pacifiers for much longer than an hour without her ingesting too much at one time, so we bought the biggest rawhide bones we could find at $10 each. The big ones kept her busy for a long time and she didn't actually swallow much.

In those first two years, the giant rawhides were a godsend. While $10 seemed a lot for one big rawhide bone, they lasted her for so long and kept her teeth so busy that they were well worth the price.

Once Dakota turned three years old she'd gotten the hang of how to peel them apart and within minutes would have a big chunk ready to swallow so we stopped offering her the big rawhides. By then she didn't need a pacifier any more.

### In training to be the perfect dog
### (Even when they're good, they're bad)

The time we put into potty training Dakota, dealing with her nervous pee issues, addressing her need to chew and teaching her which items she could legally chew on was time well invested. We had tackled her issues from many different angles, including teaching her words and playing fun games so that she wouldn't get bored and look for destructive outlets.

By the time Dakota was two years old we are able to leave her for nine hours loose in the bedroom without incident (and without chewy toys of any kind) while we were at work. This was amazing progress for a dog who initially wanted to grab everything that came into her sphere and chew on it.

The chapter entitled "Training Your Dog to be Home Alone" details how we weaned Dakota from the crate. We were up to about three hours in the main part of the house and the only incident we had was when we left a blanket on the floor. She chewed some pieces off of it. For some reason blankets on the floor defied our efforts to stop her chewing. Maybe it was a carryover from her old life. The only solution we found was to avoid leaving blankets on the floor - ever.

We were also careful not to leave small, plastic objects on the floor. I had taken a box fan apart to clean it and forgot to put the feet back on. An hour later I found them chewed to pieces.

Your dog will not go from bad to perfect overnight. The fan feet incident happened months after we thought we could trust her but such incidents were rare and they didn't happen at all if we were careful about what we left on the floor.

Dakota had learned early on not to grab things off of tables so most of our efforts were spent on things lying on the floor. We trusted her enough to leave her for many hours in a room that we'd dog-proofed for the items that tempted her. Remember, dog training is about creating new habits to replace the old ones and just as with a toddler, you may need to dog-proof your home while they are in the training stage.

# Training Your Dog to be Home Alone

*Trust this wild-eyed bucking bronco home alone?*
*(You must be NUTS!)*

If your goal is to break your dog of needing a crate when you are not at home, then read on. This is the next installment of Dakota's story: our method of weaning her from the crate. Yes, believe it or not we were successful in teaching Dakota to stay home alone with full run of the house on our workdays. For nine and a half straight hours, this dog mastered the art of being home - unsupervised - without chewing or pottying in the house. It was nothing short of a miracle (and a lot of hard work retraining her.)

Remember her wild beginnings with us when she smeared poop on everything in her reach, ripped open a bag of cement and peed on almost every inch of our carpeting? Dakota had chewed up plastic bowls, automatic water dispensers, coasters, rolls of toilet tissue, blankets, and a variety of small plastic objects. We learned early on that when left unsupervised Dakota was destructive so on our workdays she was relegated to her crate. I don't know why they call it a crate; it looks like a cage to me.

Even in the crate we did not fully trust her. We were afraid she would attempt to break out of jail so we reinforced the crate with metal clips at all the seams. In addition, we clipped the door latches. Dakota loose in the house would have been disastrous.

As it turns out our fears were not unfounded. I later read stories of dogs who did the very thing we were afraid of - forcing their way out of the crate through the seams.

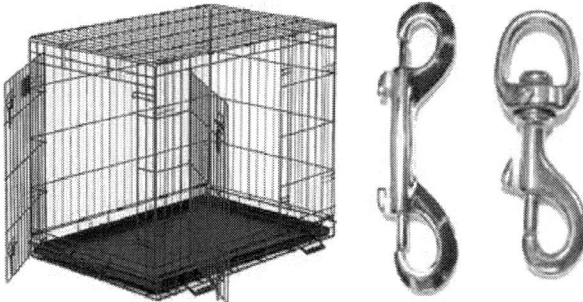

**DOG CRATE AND REINFORCEMENT CLIPS**

For us, however, the crate was a godsend. Dakota did not potty in the crate even when she was confined in it for nine hours on our workdays.

Neither did she bark. It wasn't our favorite option but we didn't have a better alternative. The crate we chose was much bigger than Dakota. She could stand up, sit up, turn around, lie down and stretch out without being cramped. The crate allowed Dakota to be in the house when we were gone and it was the first step in giving her freedom of the house.

### Freedom must be earned
### *(Out of sight, out of my mind with worry)*

Before we could undertake the next step, we had to make sure she was fully potty trained and that she wouldn't chew. You cannot expect a dog to be good when you are gone if they aren't good when you are at home.

We did not attempt to wean Dakota from her crate until we were confident that she could, and would, hold her pee, and that we could reasonably trust her not to destroy things. This phase of her dog training was very gradual. Dakota had come to us godawful so it was going to take a lot for us to trust her with this very big step. This is another area where people fail. They leave their dog home alone without first having trained the dog not to chew or pee in the house, and then they don't understand when their house gets torn apart and pottied on.

In teaching Dakota not to be bad in the house, we kept her in our sight at all times so that we could immediately deal with potty and chewing issues. If she attempted to leave whatever room we were in, we'd call her back or follow her - *just as we would have with a toddler.*

Once she stopped grabbing things illegally while in our sight she was ready to graduate to the next level. We'd let her disappear out of sight for a few minutes before following to check up on her. Baby steps - we took her dog training in baby steps. Once we knew she could be left alone for three or four minutes out of sight without incident, we'd let it go longer. Over the course of many months we began to trust her alone in other rooms as long as she was on the same floor we were on. We used a baby gate to block the stairway.

This is the first step in training a dog to be home alone with freedom in the house. First you must be able to trust them out of your sight when you are at home.

### Home alone
### *(Will bad dog trash the house?)*

Once you have achieved that goal then you can start the next phase: leaving them alone in the house when you are outside. Initially this was also for just a few minutes - I left her loose in the house when I'd go out to get the mail or empty the garbage. A dog can get into mischief that quickly so again, we took this journey with her in stages.

The next step came when a neighbor stopped me to chit chat by the mailbox - which took Dakota to the next level of 20 minutes alone in the house. Dakota spent those minutes watching me. I could see her face in the window so I did not worry overmuch.

As the weeks passed I took every small opportunity to leave Dakota alone inside: when I took out the mail, talked to a neighbor in the driveway, mowed the lawn, trimmed the roses, or any activity that put me outside for a short period of time. When we reached that golden place where she could be left indoors while we were outdoors we could then start weaning her from the crate when we were gone.

### Moving on up
### (Graduating from the crate)

She did not move from the crate to full run of the house in one step. The next goal we set out to achieve was to leave her alone in the bedroom with the door closed. She was already sleeping through the night loose in our bedroom without incident so we began to put her in the bedroom with the door closed during the day when we were at home to get her used to the idea. We did this for very brief periods. Make sure to potty the dog first so that they are empty. It's better to prevent an accident than clean one up later. It's better for them to learn the right habit from the start than to break a bad habit later.

Again we took this in steps - five minutes, then ten, then twenty, and up to forty five minutes locked in the bedroom alone. Our bedroom was for sleeping. We never played with her in there so she associated this room with sleep or lying down quietly while waiting for us to get up in the morning. We removed several things from the bedroom that we thought might tempt her before moving to this phase of training: a phone sitting on the floor, a guitar, and shoes. We did not leave any temptations for her.

### Moving into the penthouse
### (Dakota earns a gold star)

Once she was accustomed to being locked in the bedroom we started putting her in the bedroom instead of the crate if we were going out for a quick errand. When I say quick I mean *quick* - such as directly to the post office and back or the bank and back - errands which only took about a half hour start to finish. We did not put Dakota in the bedroom if we were running multiple errands or if it was possible for the errand to go longer than anticipated. You don't throw a child in the deep end of the pool without first making sure they can swim.

Once we knew we could trust her for a half hour, we upped it to one hour, then two. We started putting her in the bedroom when we went to the grocery store. We made sure not to combine errands during this phase of her training if in doing so she'd be left for longer than we felt she was ready for.

Little by little we left her in the bedroom for longer periods, always pottying her right before we left and again *immediately* when we got home. Our own personal potty could wait, putting up groceries could wait, everything could wait for us to take her out to pee because she was in a highly excited state. We'd take her out as fast as we could get her out the door, afterward giving her a really good treat and a lot of praise, and then all of us settling down to our normal routines.

Dakota quickly realized that when we left we either put her in the crate or we put her in the bedroom. We'd estimate how long we'd be gone and then decide between the two. If she was up to two hours in the bedroom and we were just going to the grocery store, then it was a bedroom day, but if we were going to a friend's house for the evening it meant we'd be gone for several hours so we put her in the crate. She had to work her way up to being left alone in the bedroom for that many hours.

Dakota fully understood that this was an option and that she didn't have to be in the crate when we left. As soon as she realized we were going somewhere she'd hightail it up the stairs and into the bedroom. She'd look at us with woeful eyes begging us to let her stay in the bedroom. It was hard. She knew that the bedroom was an option so it was hard for us to put her in the crate. It felt like we were punishing her even though she hadn't done anything wrong.

Training her to be home alone was a critical step for a dog that came to us with so many problems. We didn't want to jump too far forward too fast in her training. We couldn't give her freedom for six hours until we knew she could handle two, then three, then four, then five. As hard as it was to look her in the eye and put her in the crate we had to follow the plan diligently to ensure her success.

When we first adopted her I could not have imagined leaving her alone in the house for even one single minute. One year later she spent six hours alone in the bedroom while we were out and she aced it. I was so very proud of the progress she had made from being the most godawful dog to this incredible dog that I was learning to trust. It took another year to give her full run of the house while we were gone though she did have run of the house when we were outside.

The long delay in training her to have full run of the house was primarily because we didn't want to leave her alone with Gypsy Rose. She never gained our trust in that area so we kept them separated if we were not around to supervise.

When we attempted to put Gypsy Rose in the bedroom and let Dakota have full run of the house, both dogs felt as if they were being punished. The bedroom was Dakota's safe place and she didn't like being locked out. For Gypsy Rose the bedroom felt like punishment, so we aborted our efforts to give Dakota run of the house until Gypsy Rose passed away which was almost a year later.

Once Gypsy Rose passed away we started giving Dakota full run of the house just as we'd done with the bedroom - starting with short periods of time and then graduating to longer periods until we finally left her on a workday.

Today she routinely spends nine and a half hours alone in the house without incident - no chewing, no potty and no barking. We believe she spends most of the time snoozing in the bedroom - the room she has claimed for her safe haven. We don't even give it a thought anymore to worry about leaving her. We are so incredibly proud of her.

IN TRAINING TO BE THE PERFECT DOG

Printed in Great Britain
by Amazon